FOREX TRADING MADE EASY:
A BEGINNER'S GUIDE

By: Devon Piccinin

Devon Piccinin

Copyright © 2023 by Devon Piccinin

writing from the publisher.

Published by: Devon Piccinin
Printed in: United States of America
First Edition: 2023

Disclaimer:

The information provided in this book is for educational purposes only and does not constitute financial advice. The author and publisher are not liable for any losses or damages resulting from the use or misuse of the information presented in this book. Readers are advised to consult with a professional financial advisor before making any investment decisions.

DEDICATION

To my dearest God,

I begin this dedication with a grateful heart, for it is through your infinite grace and guidance that I have found the strength to embark on this journey of writing and sharing my knowledge. You have blessed me with the wisdom to understand the complexities of forex trading and the ability to simplify it for beginners like myself. With every word penned in this book, I aspire to honor your teachings and spread the light of knowledge to those seeking financial freedom.

In this dedication, I also express my boundless love and gratitude to my faithful companions—Missy, Daisy, Scout, and Ranger. These loyal beings have been my pillars of strength, providing unwavering support, and endless love. Their presence has brought joy, comfort, and inspiration into my life, reminding me of the preciousness of love and companionship. As I write this dedication, they lay by my side, their gentle breaths a soothing melody, reminding me of the unconditional love you pour upon me each day.

To my future family, not yet physically present but eternally rooted in my heart, I dedicate this book as a testament to the love and dreams we will share.

◆ ◆ ◆

"Success in Forex trading, like in life, requires discipline, patience, and continuous learning. Mastering the art of simplicity and embracing a strategic mindset will pave the way for abundant opportunities"

-DEVON PICCININ

TABLE OF CONTENTS

INTRODUCTION

Welcome to the exciting world of forex trading, where fortunes are made and dreams come true. If you have ever wondered how some people manage to make their money work for them, while others struggle to make ends meet, then this book is for you. In these pages, you will discover the transformative power of forex trading and how it can help you achieve your financial goals. But beware, once you delve into the world of forex, there is no going back – you will be hooked for life!

Imagine a life where you are not tied down by a 9-to-5 job, where financial freedom becomes your reality. Picture yourself traveling the world, making money from the comfort of your laptop, and achieving financial independence. This is not a mere fantasy; it is a dream that thousands of successful forex traders have turned into a reality. And now, with Forex Trading Made Easy: A Beginner's Guide, you too can join this elite group of individuals and embark on a journey to financial prosperity.

In this book, we aim to demystify forex trading and make it accessible to anyone with the desire to learn. No prior knowledge or experience is necessary – all you need is an open mind and the willingness to embark on this adventure. Whether you are a student, a stay-at-home parent, or a seasoned professional looking for a change, forex trading provides an equal opportunity platform for everyone.

First, let's address the elephant in the room – what is

forex trading? Forex, short for foreign exchange, is the global decentralized market where all the world's currencies are traded. With a daily turnover of over $6 trillion, it is by far the largest and most liquid financial market in the world. Unlike stock markets, forex trading operates 24 hours a day, five days a week, allowing traders to seize opportunities around the clock. This market is vast, dynamic, and full of potential for those who know how to navigate it effectively.

Now, you might be thinking, "But isn't forex trading complicated? Don't you need a finance degree and years of experience to excel in this field?" Absolutely not! That is the beauty of it. Thanks to technological advancements and online platforms, forex trading has become accessible to anyone with an internet connection. This book will guide you through the fundamentals of forex trading, helping you build a strong foundation of knowledge and develop the skills necessary to navigate this lucrative market.

So, what is the secret sauce to successful forex trading? It boils down to two key elements: knowledge and strategy. Without the right knowledge, you are merely gambling. But armed with the right strategies, techniques, and insights, you can make informed decisions, manage risk, and increase your chances of success. In Forex Trading Made Easy: A Beginner's Guide, we will provide you with a comprehensive overview of the forex market, explain the key terms and concepts, and guide you through proven strategies that have worked for countless traders.

Whether you are interested in short-term scalping, day trading, or longer-term swing trading, this book will equip you with the tools to make informed decisions. You will learn how to analyze charts, spot trends, identify entry and exit points, manage risk, and develop a winning mindset. We will share the secrets of top traders, proven techniques, and valuable tips and tricks, allowing you to fast-track your journey to profitability.

But forex trading is not just about numbers, charts, and graphs; it is a thrilling journey fueled by passion and resilience. Throughout this book, we will delve into real-life stories of successful forex traders who started with little to no knowledge but went on to achieve remarkable success. These stories will inspire and motivate you, showing you that anyone can succeed in this field with the right mindset and dedication.

Additionally, we will explore the psychological aspects of forex trading, as mastering your emotions is key to long-term success. You will learn to identify common pitfalls, overcome fear and greed, and develop the discipline necessary to stick to your trading plan. Understanding the psychology of trading is often the missing piece in the puzzle for many aspiring traders, and we aim to bridge that gap in this book.

Forex Trading Made Easy: A Beginner's Guide is not just a one-time read; it is a comprehensive resource that you can refer back to throughout your trading journey. We have included practical exercises, checklists, and step-by-step guides to ensure you grasp the concepts and put them into practice. Additionally, we will provide you with a list of recommended resources, tools, and websites to further enhance your trading skills.

Before we embark on this exciting journey, it is important to grasp the risks associated with forex trading. While the rewards can be substantial, it is crucial to understand that trading involves a level of risk, and there are no guarantees of profits. We will emphasize risk management throughout this book, teaching you how to protect your capital, set realistic goals, and avoid common pitfalls.

So, are you ready to dive into the world of forex trading? Are you ready to unlock the door to financial independence and potentially change your life forever? If the answer is yes, then let's get started. The path to success may not always be smooth, but with the right knowledge, strategies, and mindset, you can make forex trading work for you. Get ready for an exhilarating adventure filled with ups and downs, triumphs and setbacks, and a newfound sense of control over your financial destiny. Welcome to the world of forex trading – let the journey begin!

CHAPTER 1: THE FOUNDATION
OF FOREX TRADING

Welcome to the world of Forex trading! Whether you have stumbled upon this book out of curiosity, the desire for financial freedom, or simply because you want to learn a new skill, you have come to the right place. In this chapter, we will lay the foundation for your journey towards mastering the art of Forex trading.

But first, let's address the burning question: what exactly is Forex trading?

Forex, short for foreign exchange, refers to the global marketplace where one currency is exchanged for another. It is the largest and most liquid financial market in the world, with trillions of dollars being traded daily. Unlike the stock market, which operates in specific hours, Forex trading is open 24 hours a day, five days a week. The appeal of Forex trading lies in its accessibility and potential for profit.

Now, let's dive deeper into why Forex trading has become such a popular venture.

1. Flexibility and Freedom

Forex trading offers immense flexibility and freedom. You can trade from anywhere as long as you have an internet connection and a computer or smartphone. This means you can manage your trades while traveling the world or even from the comfort of your own home. You no longer need to be tied down to a specific location or confined by the traditional 9-to-5 job.

2. Unlimited Profit Potential

The potential for profit in Forex trading is astronomical. The value of currencies fluctuates constantly, providing ample opportunities to capitalize on price movements. If you know how to analyze the market, identify trends, and execute strategic trades, you can make substantial profits in a short amount of time. Unlike other investment options, Forex trading does not require a large capital to get started, and the profits are not limited by a fixed interest rate.

3. Level Playing Field

Forex trading is unique in that it offers a level playing field for all traders. Regardless of your educational background, experience, or financial status, anyone can participate in Forex trading. Successful traders are not limited to a select few but are determined by their skills, knowledge, and ability to adapt to market conditions. This means that you have an equal chance to succeed in this field.

Now that you understand the advantages of Forex trading, let's discuss the fundamental principles that will serve as the building blocks of your journey towards becoming a successful Forex trader.

1. Education is Key

Before diving into the world of Forex trading, it is crucial to educate yourself about the market. Trading blindly without any knowledge or understanding is a recipe for disaster and will likely lead to financial losses. Take the time to learn the basic concepts, terminology, and strategies involved in Forex trading. Familiarize yourself with various technical indicators and chart patterns that will aid you in analyzing the market. Knowledge is power, and in Forex trading, it is the key to success.

2. Develop a Trading Plan

A trading plan is a roadmap that outlines your trading goals, strategies, risk tolerance, and money management techniques. It is essential to create a solid trading plan that aligns with your personal goals and objectives. This plan will serve as a guideline that will help you make informed decisions and avoid impulsive, emotional trading. Remember, Forex trading is not about making quick, rash decisions; it is about executing well-thought-out trades based on a sound strategy.

3. Practice with Demo Accounts

Before risking your hard-earned money in the live market, it is highly recommended to practice with demo accounts. Demo accounts simulate real-time trading conditions but allow you to trade with virtual money. This gives you the opportunity to apply the knowledge and strategies you have learned without any financial risk. It is crucial to gain hands-on experience and build confidence before transitioning to live trading.

4. Emotional Control and Discipline

Emotional control and discipline are paramount in Forex trading. The market is volatile and unpredictable, and it is easy to let fear or greed cloud your judgment. Successful traders understand the importance of staying calm and rational during both winning and losing trades. They follow their trading plan meticulously and do not succumb to impulsive decisions. Developing emotional control and discipline takes time and practice, but it is essential for long-term success in Forex trading.

5. Risk Management

Risk management is a critical component of Forex trading. It involves understanding and mitigating potential losses by setting stop-loss orders and implementing proper position sizing techniques. A well-designed risk management strategy will protect your capital and prevent catastrophic losses. Remember, Forex trading is not about winning every trade, but rather minimizing losses and maximizing gains over the long run.

6. Continuous Learning and Adaptation

Forex trading is a constantly evolving field, and it is essential to stay updated with market trends, economic news, and geopolitical events that can impact currency prices. Successful traders are lifelong learners who continuously seek new knowledge, refine their strategies, and adapt to changing market conditions. Dedicate yourself to continuous learning to stay ahead of the curve and remain competitive in the Forex market.

By understanding and implementing these fundamental principles, you are laying a strong foundation for your Forex trading journey. Remember, success takes time, effort, and perseverance. Embrace the challenges, learn from your mistakes, and never stop pursuing knowledge and improvement.

In the following chapters, we will delve deeper into specific strategies, technical analysis, fundamental analysis, and other advanced concepts that will further enhance your understanding of Forex trading. Get ready to embark on an exciting and rewarding adventure that has the potential to change your financial future.

CHAPTER 2: UNVEILING THE MYSTERY

Welcome back, dear reader. Now that we have established a solid foundation in Chapter 1, it's time to take our journey into the fascinating world of Forex trading to the next level. In this chapter, we will delve into the mystical realm of Forex and unravel the mysteries that surround it. Get ready to have your mind blown and your curiosity satiated as we unveil the secrets behind this global financial market.

1. The Origins of Forex Trading

To truly understand the essence of Forex trading, we must travel back in time to trace its roots. The origins of Forex can be dated back to ancient times when different civilizations engaged in foreign currency exchange to facilitate trade. Merchants would trade their goods with others from distant lands, and to ensure fair transactions, they exchanged their respective local currencies.

The modern Forex market, as we know it today, emerged in the 1970s when the Bretton Woods Agreement collapsed. This agreement had pegged major currencies to the U.S. dollar, but its dissolution led to the birth of a floating exchange rate system. This new system allowed currencies to fluctuate based on market forces, providing a perfect breeding ground for speculative trading.

2. What is Forex Trading?

Forex, short for Foreign Exchange, refers to the buying and selling of currencies on the global market. This decentralized market operates 24/5 and is the largest and most liquid financial market in the world. The daily turnover exceeds trillions of dollars, making it a playground for traders from all walks of life.

The main objective of Forex trading is to profit from the fluctuations in currency exchange rates. Traders can buy a currency pair if they believe its value will rise in the future or sell it if they expect the value to decline. The beauty of Forex lies in its ability to provide opportunities in both rising and falling markets, allowing traders to capitalize on any market condition.

3. Market Participants: The Avengers of Forex

Imagine a bustling marketplace filled with enthusiastic traders from around the globe. This exciting marketplace is none other than the Forex market. Let's meet the key players who make up this formidable team of market participants:

- Banks and Financial Institutions: These giants of the financial world are the primary players in the Forex market. They facilitate the majority of transactions and provide liquidity to ensure smooth market operations.

- Central Banks: These governmental entities, such as the Federal Reserve and the European Central Bank, are responsible for formulating monetary policies and controlling interest rates. Their actions greatly influence currency values and, therefore, impact the Forex market.

- Hedge Funds and Investment Firms: These institutional investors manage massive funds, making strategic trades to maximize profits. Their market influence is significant, and their trading decisions can cause ripples in the Forex pond.

- Retail Traders: Here's where you, dear reader, fit in. Individual traders like yourself participate in the Forex market through online trading platforms. Though small in size compared to the giants, retail traders collectively contribute to the market's liquidity and add diversity to the trading community.

4. The ABCs of Currency Pairs

In Forex trading, currencies are traded in pairs. Each pair represents the exchange rate between two different currencies. Here are a few popular currency pairs that you'll often encounter:

- EUR/USD: Euro against the U.S. dollar
- GBP/USD: British pound against the U.S. dollar
- USD/JPY: U.S. dollar against the Japanese yen
- AUD/USD: Australian dollar against the U.S. dollar

The first currency in the pair is called the base currency, and the second currency is known as the quote currency. The value of the currency pair represents how much of the quote currency is needed to buy one unit of the base currency. For example, if the EUR/USD pair is trading at 1.20, it means that one euro can be exchanged for 1.20 U.S. dollars.

5. The Weapons of Forex Trading: Leverage and Margin

In the battle of Forex trading, leverage and margin are the powerful weapons that can amplify your gains or losses. Let's break down these concepts to ensure you can wield them effectively:

- Leverage: This financial tool allows traders to control larger positions in the market with a smaller initial investment. For example, with a 1:100 leverage, you can control a $100,000 position with just $1,000. While leverage can boost your profits, it's important to handle it with caution as it also increases the potential for losses.

- Margin: Margin refers to the collateral required by your broker to open and maintain a trading position. It is a percentage of the total trade size, and it acts as a safety net for the broker in case your trade turns against you. Always make sure to have a clear understanding of your broker's margin requirements before placing trades.

6. Diving into Technical and Fundamental Analysis

To navigate the Forex market successfully, you need a reliable compass comprised of two primary analysis methods: technical analysis and fundamental analysis. Let's explore these tools that will guide you through the murky waters of trading:

- Technical Analysis: This approach involves studying historical price charts, patterns, and indicators to predict future price movements. Traders use various tools like support and resistance levels, moving averages, and oscillators to identify potential entry and exit points for their trades.

- Fundamental Analysis: Fundamental analysis involves examining economic indicators, news events, and geopolitical factors that can impact currency prices. By analyzing factors such as interest rates, unemployment rates, and GDP growth, traders can make informed decisions about the direction of a currency pair.

7. The Quest for the Holy Grail: Developing a Trading Strategy

No knight embarks on a quest without a strategy, and the same applies to Forex trading. Developing a solid trading strategy is the key to consistent profits in this unpredictable market. Here are the essential components of a winning strategy:

- Risk Management: Before entering any trade, a successful trader assesses the potential risks and set stop-loss and take-profit levels to protect their capital. Risk management is crucial to ensure that losses are controlled and do not outweigh gains.

- Entry and Exit Rules: A trading strategy must provide clear guidelines for entering and exiting trades. This includes identifying specific criteria for entering a trade based on technical or fundamental analysis, as well as having predetermined profit targets and stop-loss levels for exiting the trade.

- Emotional Discipline: One of the greatest challenges in Forex trading is controlling emotions. Greed, fear, and impatience can cloud judgment and lead to disastrous decisions. A successful trader must have the discipline to stick to their strategy, even in the face of tempting market fluctuations.

8. The Tools of the Trade: Trading Platforms and Indicators

Equipped with your newfound knowledge, it's time to explore the tools of the trade. Trading platforms and indicators are essential instruments that assist in the execution of trading strategies. Here are some popular trading platforms and indicators:

- MetaTrader 4 (MT4) and MetaTrader 5 (MT5): These platforms are widely used by Forex traders due to their user-friendly interface, advanced charting capabilities, and a wide range of indicators and expert advisors.

- Moving Averages: Moving averages help traders identify trends by smoothing out price data over a given period. They come in different forms, such as simple moving averages (SMA) and exponential moving averages (EMA).

- Relative Strength Index (RSI): The RSI is a momentum oscillator that measures the speed and change of price movements. It helps traders identify overbought and oversold conditions in the market, providing hints for potential reversals.

9. The Psychological Battle: Mastering Your Mind

As you dive deeper into the world of Forex trading, you'll soon discover that success or failure depends not only on your technical skills but also on your mindset. The psychological battle within the trader's mind is just as crucial as any technical analysis or trading strategy. Here are some key aspects to master your mind:

- Patience and Discipline: Forex trading requires patience and discipline to wait for the right trading opportunities and stick to your strategy. Impulsive decisions based on emotions can lead to catastrophic results.

- Emotional Intelligence: Understanding and controlling your emotions is essential in trading. Being aware of your emotional state and making rational decisions is crucial to long-term success. Remember, trading is a marathon, not a sprint.

- Continuous Learning: The Forex market is constantly evolving, and as a trader, you must commit to lifelong learning. Stay updated with market news, attend webinars, read books, and engage with other traders to strengthen your knowledge and skills.

10. Your First Step: Creating a Demo Account

Now that you're armed with the knowledge of Forex trading, it's time to take your first steps into the market. But before risking your hard-earned money, it is highly recommended to create a demo account. A demo account allows you to practice trading in a risk-free environment, using virtual funds. It will help you familiarize yourself with the trading platform and test your strategies before risking real money.

Congratulations, brave reader! You have successfully unveiled the mysteries of Forex trading. In this chapter, we traveled through time, met the avengers of Forex, learned the art of analyzing markets, and discovered the tools and psychology required to conquer the trading arena. Armed with this knowledge, you are now ready to take on the challenges and reap the rewards of the Forex market. Remember, patience, discipline, and continuous learning are the keys to becoming a successful trader. Onwards to Chapter 3, where we will reveal the the art of development & relationships in forex trading mastery. Stay tuned!

CHAPTER 3: THE ART OF DEVELOPMENT & RELATIONSHIPS IN FOREX TRADING MASTERY

Congratulations on making it to Chapter 3 of "Forex Trading Made Easy: A Beginner's Guide!" By now, you have established a solid foundation in understanding the forex market, developed a winning mindset, mastered technical analysis, and honed your risk management skills. In this chapter, we will dive deep into the art of developing relationships in forex trading.

Why are relationships crucial in forex trading?

Forex trading is not just about analyzing charts, indicators, and economic news. It also involves building strong and meaningful connections with other traders, experts, and mentors. These relationships can have a profound impact on your trading journey, propelling you towards success and helping you navigate the challenges along the way. Let's explore the key reasons why relationships are crucial in forex trading mastery.

1. Mentorship and Guidance:

One of the most valuable relationships you can develop is with an experienced and successful forex trader who can act as your mentor. Having a mentor by your side gives you access to their wisdom, knowledge, and experiences, allowing you to shortcut your learning curve and avoid common pitfalls.

A mentor can provide guidance on refining your trading strategies, spotting market trends, managing risk, and overcoming psychological barriers. By learning from someone who has already traveled the path, you gain valuable insights that can accelerate your progress towards profitability.

2. Collaborative Learning:

In forex trading, no one has all the answers. It's a constantly evolving market that requires continuous learning and adaptation. This is where collaborative relationships with fellow traders come into play. Engaging in discussions, sharing ideas, and seeking constructive feedback from a community of like-minded individuals can enhance your understanding of the market.

Joining forex trading forums, attending conferences, participating in online communities, or even forming a study group with friends can all be avenues for collaborative learning. By being open to different perspectives and ideas, you gain a broader understanding of the market and increase the probability of making informed trading decisions.

3. Emotional Support:

Forex trading isn't always smooth sailing. There will be times when the market goes against you, trades don't go as planned, or losses occur. During these challenging moments, having a supportive network can be immensely beneficial to your emotional well-being.

Building relationships with traders who have been through similar experiences helps you realize that you're not alone in facing adversity. Sharing your struggles, seeking advice, and receiving words of encouragement can boost your morale and help you stay focused on your trading goals. Remember, emotional stability is a vital ingredient for long-term success in forex trading.

4. Networking Opportunities:

In any industry, networking plays a crucial role in opening doors to new opportunities. Forex trading is no exception. By building strong relationships within the trading community, you increase your chances of discovering unique opportunities, such as potential partnerships, collaborations, or even job offers within trading firms.

Attending trading conferences, industry events, or reaching out to seasoned traders can help expand your network and expose you to new ideas and perspectives. Remember to approach networking with sincerity, genuine interest, and the desire to add value to others. This way, you'll foster authentic connections that can propel your trading career forward.

Developing Relationships: Strategies and Best Practices

Now that we understand why relationships are crucial in forex trading, let's explore some strategies and best practices to develop meaningful connections within the trading community.

1. Seek Mentorship:

Finding a mentor can significantly accelerate your learning curve and enhance your trading skills. Look for experienced traders who align with your trading style, goals, and values. Reach out to them respectfully, expressing your admiration for their work and asking if they would be open to guiding you. Be proactive in your learning journey and take advantage of the valuable insights your mentor provides.

2. Join Online Communities:

The internet has made it easier than ever to connect with traders from all around the world. Join online communities, such as trading forums, social media groups, or specialized platforms, to engage in discussions, share knowledge, and seek guidance.

Be an active participant by asking thoughtful questions, sharing your experiences, and supporting others. Remember, relationships are a two-way street, and contributing your expertise and insights can help solidify your position within the community.

3. Attend Trading Meetups and Conferences:

Search for local trading meetups or attend industry conferences where you can meet like-minded individuals face-to-face. These events provide invaluable opportunities to network, learn from experts, and build relationships in a more personal setting.

Embrace the chance to engage in conversations, exchange business cards, and follow up with individuals whose discussions resonate with you. Fostering connections in person can leave a lasting impression and open doors to collaborations or mentorship opportunities.

4. Be Authentic and Genuine:

Authenticity and genuineness are key when aiming to establish lasting relationships. People are more likely to connect with someone who is sincere and transparent. Be honest about your strengths, weaknesses, and experiences. Avoid pretending to be someone you're not or exaggerating your successes. This way, you attract individuals who appreciate you for who you are and build trust within the trading community.

5. Embrace Continuous Learning:

The forex market is constantly evolving, so it's essential to stay updated with the latest trends and trading strategies. Attend webinars, read relevant books and articles, and enroll in advanced trading courses. By continuously expanding your knowledge and skillset, you position yourself as a valuable asset in the trading community and attract meaningful relationships.

In the world of forex trading, developing and nurturing relationships is a crucial aspect of achieving mastery. Whether it's seeking mentorship, collaborating with fellow traders, receiving emotional support, or accessing networking opportunities, relationships play a significant role in enhancing your trading journey.

Remember, relationships thrive on mutual respect, trust, and genuine interest in adding value to others. Be proactive, seek guidance, share your experiences, and contribute to the broader trading community. By engaging in the art of development and relationships, you will unlock a world of possibilities and accelerate your path to forex trading mastery. Happy networking!

CHAPTER 4: UNLOCKING THE HIDDEN SECRETS OF FOREX TRADING

Welcome to the exhilarating world of Forex trading, where every twist and turn holds the promise of unimaginable wealth or devastating loss. In this chapter, we will delve deep into the realm of plot twists and surprises in Forex trading. Brace yourself as we unveil the hidden secrets that will enable you to navigate this unpredictable landscape, turning every surprise into an opportunity to profit.

The Element of Surprise in Forex Trading

1.1 The Art of Anticipation:

Imagine the excitement of watching a thrilling movie, not knowing what will happen next. Similarly, Forex trading is an adventure where surprises are aplenty. Successful traders understand the importance of anticipation - the ability to predict and prepare for dramatic plot twists that the market throws their way.

1.2 Uncovering the Unexpected:

In Forex trading, surprises can come in various forms. It could be an unexpected economic event, a sudden policy change, or a market manipulation. The most skilled traders are masters at uncovering the unexpected and turning it to their advantage. Throughout this chapter, we will explore these surprises and reveal strategies to exploit them.

Economic Events

2.1 The Power of Economic Indicators:

Economic indicators can send shockwaves through the Forex market, catching unprepared traders off guard. In this section, we will examine key economic indicators such as GDP, inflation rates, and employment reports. More importantly, we will unveil strategies to anticipate and profit from the surprises these indicators bring.

2.2 Central Bank Surprises:

Central banks hold immense power in shaping Forex markets with their monetary policies. Unforeseen decisions, interest rate changes, or unexpected announcements can send currencies on a rollercoaster ride. Discover the secrets to deciphering the hidden messages of central banks and how to ride the wave of their surprises.

2.3 Political Events: The Ultimate Plot Twist

Political events, such as elections and referendums, have the potential to create seismic shifts in currency values. We will delve into recent historical examples like Brexit and the U.S. presidential elections, exploring how political surprises can redefine the market landscape. Learn how to spot political plot twists before they unfold and make wise trading decisions.

Manipulating the Market - The Dark Side of Forex Trading

3.1 Insider Trading and Market Manipulation:

Ah, the plot twist that can send shockwaves through the trading community - market manipulation. Dark forces may attempt to sway the market in their favor, leaving ordinary traders bewildered. Discover the telltale signs of manipulation and the strategies to profit from these unexpected maneuvers, turning the tables on the manipulators themselves.

3.2 Pump and Dump: The Classic Twist:

The notorious "Pump and Dump" scheme has plagued the financial markets for years. Unscrupulous traders artificially inflate the value of a currency before selling it off, leaving unsuspecting traders in the dust. Uncover the psychology behind these manipulations and gain the upper hand by catching these plot twists before they unfold.

3.3 Black Swan Events - The Unpredictable Surprise:

Black Swan events refer to highly improbable, yet incredibly impactful surprises. From natural disasters to global economic downturns, these events can shake the foundations of the Forex market. We will examine famous Black Swan events of the past and provide practical advice on how to protect yourself and even capitalize on these unpredictable twists of fate.

Embracing the Unexpected - Turning Surprises into Profits

4.1 Adapt or Perish:

In the midst of sudden plot twists and surprises, the ability to adapt becomes the trader's most valuable asset. We will explore mindset shifts, risk management techniques, and strategies to embrace and capitalize on unexpected market movements.

4.2 The Power of Technical Analysis:

Technical analysis can be a trader's guiding light when the unexpected strikes. Learn to identify key support and resistance levels, spot trends, and interpret indicators amidst market surprises. Armed with these tools, you will be able to dance through the sea of surprises with grace and precision.

4.3 Creating a Safety Net: Hedging and Diversification:

No trader can predict every plot twist in the Forex market, but with proper risk management techniques, you can build a safety net. We will unveil the secrets of hedging, diversification, and position-sizing strategies that will help protect your capital and reduce the impact of unexpected surprises.

Congratulations! You have now unlocked the hidden secrets of plot twists and surprises in Forex trading. Armed with the knowledge and strategies from this chapter, you are ready to navigate the unpredictable twists and turns of the Forex market. Remember, in this thrilling adventure, surprises are not your enemies but lucrative opportunities waiting to be seized. Brace yourself, stay vigilant, and let the surprises come.

CHAPTER 5: UNLEASHING THE POWER OF FOREX TRADING STRATEGIES

Congratulations, dear reader! You have come a long way on your journey to mastering the art of Forex trading. By now, you have acquired an in-depth understanding of essential concepts, honed your analytical skills, and discovered the importance of risk management. In this thrilling chapter, we will take your trading prowess to the next level by unraveling the secrets of highly effective Forex trading strategies.

The Anatomy of a Successful Trading Strategy

Imagine being equipped with a powerful and proven trading strategy that consistently generates profitable trades while minimizing risks. Sound too good to be true? Well, it's not! The key lies in understanding the essential elements that make up such a strategy.

1.1 Identifying Your Trading Style:

Every successful trader possesses a unique trading style that aligns with their personality, risk tolerance, and time commitment. Whether you prefer the excitement of day trading or the patience of swing trading, knowing your style will help determine which Forex strategy suits you best. Remember, there is no one-size-fits-all approach in Forex; finding your niche is the secret ingredient to success.

1.2 Setting Clear Goals:

Having a clear set of goals is crucial for any endeavor, and Forex trading is no exception. Are you aiming for short-term profits or long-term wealth accumulation? Are you looking to make a full-time income from trading or simply supplement your existing job? Defining your goals will guide you in choosing the appropriate strategy and timeframe that align with your aspirations.

1.3 Technical vs. Fundamental Analysis:

Great traders don't rely solely on one type of analysis; they understand the importance of both technical and fundamental analysis in forming their strategies. Technical analysis involves studying price charts, patterns, and indicators to identify potential entry and exit points. On the other hand, fundamental analysis scrutinizes economic and geopolitical events to predict currency movements. A combination of both approaches is often the winning formula.

Mastering Popular Forex Trading Strategies

Now that you have grasped the fundamental aspects of a successful trading strategy, it's time to explore some of the most popular and effective strategies utilized by professional traders worldwide.

2.1 Trend Following Strategy:

Trend is your friend in Forex trading, and this strategy capitalizes on identifying and trading in the direction of persistent trends. By following the market's momentum, trend followers aim to capture significant profits during sustained upward or downward movements. Learn how to spot trends, confirm them with technical indicators, and ride the wave of profits with this powerful strategy.

2.2 Breakout Strategy:

Price movements are not always smooth and predictable. Breakout traders thrive on identifying key levels of support and resistance and waiting for a breakout—when price breaches these levels—to enter a trade. This strategy thrives on volatility and seeks to capture sizable profits when the market breaks out of its range. Discover how to identify and validate breakouts, set appropriate entry and exit points, and ride the wave of momentum for impressive gains.

2.3 Range Trading Strategy:

In Forex, the market often enters periods of consolidation, called ranges, where price bounces between defined levels. Range traders profit from such market conditions by buying at the lower end of the range and selling at the upper end, thus capitalizing on multiple cycles of price oscillation. Learn how to identify ranges, confirm them with technical indicators, and profit from the repetitive nature of price movements.

Honing Your Trading Skills

It's not enough to learn about different trading strategies; successful traders continuously refine their skills to adapt to changing market conditions and enhance their decision-making abilities. In this section, we explore essential elements that will sharpen your trading edge.

3.1 Money Management:

Risk management is the cornerstone of successful Forex trading, and mastering money management is essential to preserve your capital while maximizing profits. Learn how to determine the appropriate lot size per trade, set stop-loss and take-profit levels, and effectively manage your trading account to achieve consistent long-term gains.

3.2 Emotional Mastery:

Trading can be an emotional rollercoaster, and emotional decision-making often leads to poor trading outcomes. Developing emotional mastery is crucial for maintaining discipline, managing stress, and making rational trading decisions. Discover practical techniques to control your emotions, overcome fear and greed, and stay focused on your trading plan.

3.3 Backtesting and Forward Testing:

Wouldn't it be great to test your trading strategy without risking real money? That's where backtesting and forward testing come into play. Backtesting involves analyzing historical data to evaluate the performance of your strategy, while forward testing allows you to simulate trades in real market conditions. Learn how to leverage these testing methods to ensure your strategy's effectiveness before risking your hard-earned capital.

By reaching this chapter, you have proven your commitment to becoming a successful Forex trader. With a solid understanding of trading strategies and the skills to implement them, you are now armed with the knowledge to navigate the exhilarating world of Forex trading. Remember, trading is a journey, and constant learning, practice, and adaptation are what will drive you towards enduring success. Embrace the challenge, trust the process, and let your trading strategies propel you towards your financial dreams!

EPILOGUE

Congratulations! You have reached the end of Forex Trading Made Easy: A Beginner's Guide, and by now, you should feel more confident and knowledgeable about the world of forex trading. You have learned about the basics, the strategies, and the mindset required to succeed in this exciting financial market. I hope that this book has inspired you to embark on a captivating journey towards financial independence and a brighter future.

As we conclude this guide, I want to remind you of the important lessons we have covered and provide you with some final words of encouragement and guidance.

Reflecting on Your Progress

Take a moment to reflect on how far you have come since the beginning of your forex trading journey. You started with little or no knowledge, and now you possess a solid foundation of understanding. Remember, learning never stops in the world of trading, so make sure to continue developing your skills, testing new strategies, and staying up-to-date with the latest market trends.

Embracing Continuous Learning

Forex trading is a dynamic field that requires continuous learning to adapt to the ever-changing market conditions. Stay curious, invest in education, read books, attend workshops, and engage with fellow traders to deepen your understanding. Even experienced traders with many years of successful trading continue to learn and refine their skills. As Arthur C. Clarke once said, "The greatest tragedy in life is the unlived life, and the greatest joy is the life lived in pursuit of excellence, purpose, and contribution."

Setting Realistic Goals

Set achievable goals for yourself and your trading journey. Remember, success in forex trading is not an overnight achievement. It requires patience, perseverance, and disciplined practice. Start with small, achievable goals and gradually increase your targets as you gain experience. Setting realistic goals will allow you to celebrate small wins along the way, maintaining motivation and momentum.

Building Your Trading Plan

It is critical to have a well-defined trading plan that suits your personality and trading style. Your plan should outline your goals, risk management strategies, trading tools, and analysis techniques. It should also include guidelines on when to enter and exit trades. Remember to review and adapt your trading plan based on your experiences and the evolving market conditions. A trading plan is not set in stone; it is a living document that should be updated and refined as needed.

Mastering Risk Management

As we emphasized throughout this book, risk management is the bedrock of successful trading. Minimize your exposure to risk by setting stop-loss orders, utilizing proper position sizing, diversifying your trading portfolio, and avoiding emotional decision-making. Never risk more than you can afford to lose, and always prioritize the preservation of your capital over chasing profits. As Warren Buffett wisely said, "Rule No.1: Never lose money. Rule No.2: Never forget Rule No.1."

Developing the Right Mindset

Trading is as much about psychology as it is about numbers and analysis. Cultivate a mindset that allows you to remain calm, disciplined, and focused while trading. Emotional control, patience, and the ability to learn from both successes and failures are essential qualities for a professional trader. Remember that losses are a part of the trading process and should be treated as valuable learning opportunities rather than failures.

Joining a Community

It is crucial to connect with other traders and surround yourself with like-minded individuals who can support and inspire you along your trading journey. Join online forums, participate in trading communities, or find a mentor who can provide guidance and share their experiences. A strong network of traders can offer valuable insights, accountability, and a sounding board for new ideas.

Innovating and Adapting

Forex trading, like any other industry, is constantly evolving. New trading strategies, tools, and technologies are being developed, and market dynamics are subject to change. Stay open-minded, be willing to adapt to new methodologies, and embrace technology-enabled trading advancements. Remember, those who fail to innovate are often left behind. Keep learning, experimenting, and adapting to stay ahead of the curve.

Balancing Work and Life

While it is important to dedicate time and effort to trading, it is equally important to maintain a healthy work-life balance. Forex trading provides flexibility, but it can also consume your time and energy if not managed properly. Prioritize self-care, spend time with loved ones, engage in hobbies, exercise regularly, and take breaks from the screens to avoid burnout. A balanced lifestyle will support your mental and emotional well-being, ultimately contributing to your success as a trader.

Continuing the Journey

Forex Trading Made Easy: A Beginner's Guide is just the starting point of your lifelong forex trading journey. It has equipped you with the fundamental knowledge and skills necessary to navigate the market, but success will require ongoing commitment, practice, and adaptation. Approach each trading day as a fresh opportunity to learn, grow, and improve. Remember, the markets can be challenging, but with the right mindset, education, and perseverance, you have the potential to achieve financial freedom.

I wish you the best of luck and tremendous success in all your future trades. May your profits be abundant, your losses be minimal, and your journey in forex trading be fulfilling and profitable.

Happy trading!

Your Fellow Trader